Draft Horse Images

Draft Horse Images

By
Robert A. Mischka

Heart Prairie Press
Whitewater, Wisconsin

Published by
Heart Prairie Press
P O Box 332
Whitewater, WI 53190

Publisher's Cataloging in Publication Data
      Mischka, Robert A.
          Draft horse images: a heavy horse photo album, 1992/93 / by Robert. A. Mischka,
          p. cm.
          ISBN 1-882199-03-0

          1. Draft Horses--Pictorial works.   I. Title.
SF311.M57 1994   636.1'5

Printed in Hong Kong

Front Cover: The Everett Black team of Belgian Geldings entering the ring at the North American Belgian Championship II show in Lexington, Kentucky.

Back Cover: Phil Roy of Mabel, Minnesota, bringing in bundles with his team of Belgian geldings, Tom and Pat.

Introduction

My first book, *Draft Horses Today*, was well received so I decided to try another. In *Draft Horse Images* I have used a photo essay approach to tell fewer stories, but in more detail than was possible in the earlier book.

The photos in this book were, with very few exceptions, taken during 1992 and 1993. They depict some of the people and events I followed during those years in my search for photos for our Draft Horse Calendar.

Robert Mischka
August, 1994

Table of Contents

Milwaukee Circus Parade

C. P. "Chappie" Fox, while Director of the Circus World Museum in Baraboo, Wisconsin, tracked down and acquired scores of rare circus wagons, usually in various stages of neglect and ruin. He had them restored and they have now become the backbone of the Museum. Chappie was not content, however, to have them enjoyed by just the Museum visitors — he wanted to share them with the whole world. He dreamed of a modern re-enactment of the old circus parade (a promotional activity which took place in the morning to stimulate ticket sales for the afternoon and evening performances) as a way to showcase these beautiful wagons. Through the generosity and fund raising efforts of Ben Barkin, a Milwaukee public relations executive, this dream has become a reality. The July Great Circus Parade in Milwaukee is now one of the major draft horse events of North America, with over 300 draft horses and 400 riding horses and ponies replicating a genuine turn-of-the-century circus parade.

The organizers of the Great Circus Parade have taken great pains to keep it as authentic as possible. The costumes and all the units, from ponies through draft and riding horses to camels and elephants, are all based on actual historical parades. One major exception has been the use of many Belgian horses in the parade as the old circuses used dapple grey Percherons almost exclusively.

C. P. "Chappie" Fox, father of the Great Circus Parade in Milwaukee.

Each year the parade organizers come up with some new attraction so that the event does not become "old hat". The 40-horse hitch was one such item, and it has now become one of the trademarks of the parade. Another year it was a new giraffe wagon. Still another and it was a random hitch of 13 Percherons in single file. The staging area for the parade has become a showground including a performing circus and other outside entertainment. The parade has become a week-long celebration — a reunion for circus and draft horse people alike.

Years ago, when we drove our own horses in the parade, I thought of it primarily as a horse event. I even complained about the lack of recognition the teamsters seemed to get in the stories and publicity about the parade. I was wrong. The horses are necessary — even essential — but this is primarily a celebration of the circus and the historic circus wagons. Having said that, for the purpose of this story we will focus on the horses and teamsters who add so much history to the event.

Jacqueline Mischka watches a team pull the Lion & Tiger Tableau circus wagon at the Circus World Museum grounds in Baraboo, Wisconsin. The Museum features a small circus and many circus acts in addition to their collection of antique circus wagons. It's definitely worth a stop if you are ever in the area.

Mr. Ben Barkin stands in front of the Pawnee Bill Wild West Bandwagon. It is through Mr. Barkin's generosity and hard work that the Circus Parade has become a continuing reality. Photo by Jim Morrill.

My good friend Neil Cox, a renowned wood sculptor from Ingersoll, Canada, stands before the figure which he restored on the United States Bandwagon. As with most events of this type, the planning, costume-making, restoration, and other work which makes the parade a success goes on all year long.

10

The Circus Parade festivities start a full week before the actual parade with the loading of the wagons on flatcars at the Circus World Museum in Baraboo. The wagons are pulled up a ramp and down a line of these special circus flatcars by a team of grey Percherons. The wagons are then blocked and tied down for their trip to Milwaukee. This is the Snake Den wagon from the Ringling Bros Circus built in the first decade of the 20th century.

The loaded train takes a two-day trip through southern Wisconsin and northern Illinois, making many stops along the way, on its way to the Milwaukee lakefront showgrounds. This picture makes it look like a lonely journey, but it is far from that. Crowds of people come out to meet the train at all the city stops, and at many rural crossings.

There are four performances of the Big-Top circus at the Parade Showgrounds each day, from Wednesday through Saturday, during parade week. I thought that today's kids would find circus acts "tame stuff" after what they see on TV, but I was wrong. Here is Mary Mischka with her two grand-daughters, Jennifer and Jacqueline, enjoying the performance.

An overall view of the Circus Parade Showgrounds at the Milwaukee lakefront. The Showgrounds include the tents with the parade draft horses, a Big-Top circus, free midway thrill acts, free petting zoo and menagerie, elephant and camel rides, and a close-up look at 70 historic circus wagons.

On Saturday, the day before the parade, each of the draft hitches must do a practice run on the showgrounds. The public is allowed to watch and get a really close-up look at the horses. Above: Merle Fischer practices with his 13 horse random hitch, a re-creation of an actual hitch done with this same wagon some 100 years ago. Below: Darrell Stair is hooking to the Charging Tiger Tableau Wagon with plenty of folks keeping an eye on how he is doing.

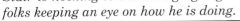

Pete Lippitt has just hitched his six, and is taking one last look at the way they are working and bitted before climbing on the seat for his practice run.

Left: A group of lucky people had tickets to ride on the Two Hemispheres Wagon during the practice run, pulled by the 40 horse hitch. It's a long way up to the top of that wagon, and the riders had to be helped by someone else who placed their feet on the steps on the wagon side.

A little girl examines the Two Hemispheres Wagon. This gives some id of the size of this, the bigg wagon in the parade. It wa built in 1903, and at 28 feet long it is the world's large bandwagon.

Paul Sparrow

Paul Sparrow drives his 40 horse hitch of Belgians back to the showgrounds at the end of the parade. At this point the parade is technically over, but Paul, his crew, and the band continue to dress, drive, and act as though they are still on national TV, much to the delight of those who watch the end of the parade from this bridge-eye view.

Paul Saetveit Photo

Just two of the many clowns who entertain the crowd before, during, and after the parade.

Gary Soule walks the parade route on his stilts.

This young lady is drawing chalk circles on the street before the parade starts to mark the spots where she expects horse-apples to appear. Actually, since the parade has over 700 horses, camels, and elephants her chances of guessing right are excellent.

Which is why these yellow beauties are the last units in the parade.

Four pinto draft horses owned and driven by Lowell Clark of Estancia, New Mexico, pulled this covered wagon. This is the very same wagon that was used by the Miller Brothers 101 Real Wild West show back in 1926. These horses are interesting both for their color and for their sex. The right wheeler is a 2-yr-old stallion, the right leader is a 13-yr-old stallion, and the other two are a mare and a gelding. The magnificent tower in the background is part of the historic Milwaukee City Hall.

Six Belgians owned and driven by Lyle Getschman of Baraboo, Wisconsin, pull the Giraffe Den Wagon containing Leitzel, a 4-month-old baby giraffe.

17

The four-abreast of greys is owned by Bill Meyer, who is sitting alongside the driver, Dick Savatski. The other four is owned and driven by Ed Moritz. Both pictures were taken as the horses were pulling the wagon up a hill. The man walking behind the wagon is holding a block fastened to the end of a pole behind the rear wheel as a safety precaution to hold the wagon from rolling backwards if the team should have to stop while on the hill.

Here we see two black Percheron eights. The top hitch is owned by Harold Schumacher, who is sitting in the center with Rick Riemer driving. The bottom hitch is owned and being driven, by Roy Fox with his brother, Larry, leaning over to give a hand with the lines.

Above: The Schlitz Bandwagon is a new wagon, built in 1972. It was first used in the Circus Parade in 1973 when it was pulled by the 40 horse hitch driven by Dick Sparrow, the second year of the 40 horse hitch and the last year the parade was sponsored by the Jos. Schlitz Brewing Co. Here it is being pulled by eight Clydes owned and driven by Merle Brooks of Westby, Wisconsin in the 1991 parade.

At the beginning of the parade, before the authentic Circus Parade begins, there is a Prelude section with beautiful vintage cars and this antique pumper wagon from the Cedarburg (Wisconsin) Fire Department.

Chappie Fox has two great passions in his life — the Circus and horses. He was able to combine both in the Great Circus Parade. In this 1967 photo he is talking with Orval Pierce (left) and Dick Sparrow (center), two of the teamsters who had driven in the parade from the beginning. Once the parade was established there was a backlog of teamsters who wanted to participate. Chappie knew them all, and established close relationships with many. He understood the importance of the horses and the teamsters to the success of the parade. "Imagine our glorious Circus Parade with all the wagons pulled by tractors put-putting down the street. The public would hate it…" Chappie would say. When new drivers were needed he got references from other teamsters before adding them. The excellent safety record of the parade is a testament to the care that has been exercised in selecting the teamsters.

Another view of the Two Hemispheres Bandwagon which gives a better idea of just how big this wagon really is. Just try counting all the musicians and teamsters that ride on this beautiful wagon.

For many years we pulled the Temple Tableau Wagon with our Mischka Farm Percherons. Here I am driving with my son, Justin, riding alongside. The lady riding on the seat in the wagon is Barbara Woodcock, a noted animal trainer with a live leopard on a leash. Barbara played to the crowd, and they responded by calling out to her by name. It was a real high. The last year we drove in the parade the leopard and Barbara were replaced by a young man and woman who were married while riding on the wagon as we travelled through the streets of downtown Milwaukee. The Temple Tableau Wagon is now pulled by 8 camels.

This is the Golden Age of Chivalry Wagon, built for Barnum & Bailey in 1903 — one of the most elaborate wagons in the parade. It is being pulled by six Shires owned and being driven by Carl Moulton of Lebanon, New Hampshire.

This is Craig Grange driving his eight Belgians hooked to the Ringling Brothers Bell Wagon, built in 1892. Riding with Craig is Harold McMain.

Kenneth Koester drives his four Percherons hooked to the Living Longhorn Tableau Wagon, replicating the 1912 parade float of the 101 Ranch Real Wild West show. Yes, that is a giant longhorn steer riding in the back of this wagon. Are you starting to get the idea? We could go on and on, with other hitches pulling wagons containing elephants, hippos, bears, giant snakes, and many other beasts. But we will leave it here, and suggest that you either come to Milwaukee to see the pageant or catch it on Public Television.

Three scenes of corn cultivating in West Central Wisconsin. The farmer at the top is using four horses on a four-row cultivator. At the right a handsome team pulls a conventional two-row cultivator. The peaceful scene at the bottom illustrates the gently rolling land that adapts very well to horse-farming.

Horse-farming

Horse-farming takes many forms. For some it means doing things the same way they were done 60 years ago, with equipment meant to be pulled by horses. For others the horses are simply a means to move their modern power-forecart and modern power-take-off equipment from field to field.

Today's power-forecarts range from homemade platforms containing a gasoline engine and an automobile seat on up to the Teamster 2000, a modern unit with ground-driven hydraulics and power-takeoff. Some of the home-made power-forecarts are actually tractors in disguise, the only difference being that they are not self-propelled and cannot be steered from the seat. Horses are used to drag them to where they are needed and to steer them.

Picking up loose hay near Richland Center, Wisconsin, with a team of young, flashy horses. The hay was not fully dried as it was being put into a silo.

A lovely sorrel team pulling a large load of dry hay. It takes three people to load a wagon like this, one to drive and two to stack and move the hay. I say this not as a criticism, but just to point out the social, economic, and employment advantages over haying with one person and a kick-baler.

Forecarts, especially power-forecarts, may represent progress but they aren't very picturesque. Given a choice I will photograph the farmer using more traditional equipment.

There are some "non-Amish" folks who use horses to farm, or to do some jobs on their farm, but the vast majority of horse-farmers are Amish or Mennonite, with religious and cultural reasons for doing so. This is both an opportunity and a difficulty for someone looking for draft horse farming photos.

The opportunity comes because Amish folks live in communities, and when you visit that community at the right time of year you can almost be assured of seeing farmers using horses in their fields. The difficulty is that Amish, as a general rule, do not want to be photographed. When I see an Amish horse-farming scene which I want to photograph I usually first walk out into the field and ask the farmer if I can take pictures of his horses. If children are driving the horses in the field I drive in the farmer's yard and ask their father the same question. The responses vary, but usually, when I make it clear I am primarily interested in just the horses, they agree. It is probably more than just a coincidence that the teams I want to photograph (because they are clean and well fed) are also those of which the owner is proud, and is pleased to have photographed.

Most Amish farming communities are prosperous, with large houses and neat farmsteads surrounded by well-kept gardens. The people are good neighbors, usually quick to stop their work for a wave or a chat. It is unfortunate that when Amish begin to move into an area there is often a feeling of resentment from their "English" residents. This is often due to the fewer number of children in the schools (Amish children go to their own country schools) and to less business for the town merchants (Amish farmers use little or no farm chemicals, produce much of their own food, sew their own clothes, etc.).

But the smaller farms, larger families, and less mechanization found in an Amish community are rays of sunshine compared to the dead and disappearing small towns that seem to be more and more the rule throughout rural Midwest. There is a lesson to be learned here, but it is being taught and told by others in their books and publications so I will let it go, and move on to some pictures.

This team of two-year olds have had their tails docked in anticipation of being sold as hitch horses when they are a little older. The hitch gelding market provides a steady stream of cash for the horse-farming community.

27

*Cutting weed
in Holmes
County, Ohio*

Loading loose hay on a flatbed wagon with no sides is hard work. Your footing is soft and moving, the hay keeps coming, and it doesn't pay to throw the hay off the wagon. Sometimes the amount of hay on the last round is a little more than you would like, but you go ahead and put it on. These horses are in good condition.

Two Amish farms, one in Wisconsin (left) and one in Ohio (above). The Amish farmhouses are large, neat, and plain. There are often several homes on a farm to accommodate the extended family.

Spring plowing on hilly land near Cashton, Wisconsin, with the ever-present farm dog following.

Two views of an Amish barn-raising, a community affair that proves the adage that many hands make the work go faster. I counted 36 men working in the picture on the right. Until I came across this scene I was wondering why there were so few farmers in their fields on that day.

Picking up soybean bundles near Littleton, Iowa. The beans are then run through a threshing machine, just like oats.

A cornfield partly shocked and partly standing. The team waits patiently while the farmer, hidden in the standing corn, picks and husks the corn and tosses the ears in the wagon. The birds circle overhead waiting their turn to do some harvesting of their own.

Merle Fisher is a dairyfarmer from Jefferson, Wisconsin, who uses modern machinery for most of his farming but likes to harvest his oats "the old way".

This was a really big load of bundles, as this field was quite far from the threshing machine and they didn't want to come back for another load.

Raking third crop alfalfa hay with two teams near New Haven, Indiana.

Mowing hay on the Bruce Coen farm near Luck, Wisconsin.

Gail Deets is a retired dairy farmer who lives on a farm near Millidgeville, Illinois, and has done so for the past 70 years. Gail quit dairying in 1977, when he was 56. He still has some horses and still farms the land, preferring to do some of the jobs with horses. Here he is off to do some corn planting, with an extra bag of seed corn under him, on the planter seat.

Gail's corn planter is a far cry from the computer-monitored monsters that are used to plant corn, apply herbicide, and deposit fertilizer today, and which have to be driven down the highway sideways.

Gail is planting his corn with Maude and Molly, a team of Belgian/Percheron cross mares. He thinks this is the best team for planting he has ever owned — they move along so nice and steady. Gail manures the fields he plants to corn and finds he needs no commercial fertilizer. This field had an excellent yield in 1991 without any chemical fertilizer or herbicides.

Gail plants his corn "with a wire". A knotted wire running the length of the field trips the planter at constant intervals, and the corn comes up in hills that can be cultivated crosswise as well as lenthwise in the row. You can see the Knotted wire along the right side of the planter in the picture at the right. The photo above shows the knotted wire being held by two sets of rollers, passing through an upright, forked arm. The knot pulls the arm back, moving the plates in the bottom of the planter box and dropping the seed. The wire, and this field, are 80 rods (1/2 mile) long.

Gail adds the sorrel son of the center mare when cultivating his corn. This is the second cultivation for this field, and he is going crosswise in the field. You can see the hills of corn in the row. He will make one more pass through this field, going the other way — the way he went when planting.

When Gail was six years old he used a cultivator just like this one, in this same field. His older sister had to come along to pull down the levers which lift the cultivator shovels at the end of the row as Gail was too small to reach them.

Gail combines his grain, but so that he will have some bundles to thresh for his Old Fashioned Farming Days (page 144) he gets the binder out and makes a few rounds.

Loading loose hay with a mixed team on an Amish farm in central Wisconsin.

Three scenes in Southwestern Wisconsin. Many horse-farmers will use horses of different colors and breeds in their operation. Good horses come in all colors and breeds.

Another farmer who prefers to harvest his oats with a binder and threshing machine is Judson Schrick, Decorah, Ia.

Judson's team are registered Belgians called Flossie and Duke.

Tom Horan was on hand the day I was there to help toss the bundles into the 22" Hart Carter threshing machine. Their collie dog is named John Deere, but they call him John for short.

Craig Grange practices with his tandem hitch on the Horse Park grounds.

Kim Sigmon drives the Windmill Acres six out of the ring, accompanied by her husband, John Sigmon.

A view of the Coliseum at the Kentucky Horse Park in which the Belgian Championship II Show was held.

North American Belgian Championship II

Kentucky Horse Park in Lexington, Kentucky, was the site of The North American Belgian Championship II. It was a memorable affair, made all the more so by beautiful September (1992) weather and the delightful Horse Park surroundings.

Approximately 500 show horses and 100 pulling horses combined to make this the largest gathering of Belgians in the memory of anyone now living. The next such show will be held in Canada in 1996, and four years later, in the year 2000, the United States should be hosting the North American Belgian Championship IV show.

The Main Entrance Gate to the Kentucky Horse Park in Lexington, Kentucky. This is a beautiful place, entirely devoted to the horse. If ever you have a chance to go there — go.

The Kentucky Horse Park consists of 1,000 acres surrounded by 27 miles of white board fence. In this single pasture you will see all five major (American) draft breeds, plus a few mules.

The halter classes were just huge, with 51 yearling mares, 46 filly foals, 47 two-year-old mares and even 7 aged stallions. The hitch classes were so large that most classes had to be split, some in thirds, with the best coming back for a final workout. This doubled the pleasure for the spectators, but also doubled the work for the exhibitors.

Paul Sparrow brought the Coors six horse hitch of Belgian geldings to the show, delighting the crowd with his docking maneuvers and galloping circles. Twenty three breeding stallions were stalled in Stallion Row, and were paraded in the coliseum for the spectators' enjoyment.

Visitors to the Horse Park had also many other attractions to enjoy, including the world-class International Museum of the Horse, an excellent driving competition, a polo match on Sunday, an Artists-in-the-Park festival on Saturday, horse-drawn trolley rides and much more.

We always hope for large crowds from the *General Public* at shows like this, but it seldom happens. There were a few folks that came to see the Country Hitch, after reading about it in one of the Reiman magazines, and a few more that came from the surrounding area — but the vast majority of the people in the stands were already "members" of the draft horse community. The general public finds our halter classes tedious and dull. Even the trot, walk, trot, reverse, trot, walk, line-up and back of the hitch classes becomes old-hat after a few days.

The judges at Lexington were, from left to right, Steve Lewis (hitches), Bob Whisman (youth), and Jim Westbrook (halter).

The public will come to see a horsepull. Horsepulls are quantitative contests of strength which the public understands. Unless we begin to include more events which involve speed, danger, agility, timing, or strength the people who attend our shows will continue to be, for the most part, the already converted. A show like the North American Championship becomes more a celebration and party for the draft horse community than a showcase and promotional activity aimed at the general public.

E. J. G. Barb was named Grand Champion Mare. Barb is owned by John Leask of Seagrave, Ontario, and was shown by Don Lowes. This mare went on to be undefeated in 1993, winning Grand Champion honors at the Royal Winter Fair, the Canadian National Exposition, and the Indiana State Fair.

H.B. Victory Supreme was named Grand Champion Stallion, repeating his earlier win at the National Belgian Show. Supreme is owned by Hale Brothers of Lovington, Illinois. Here Jack Hale leads him back to the Hale Brothers stalls. Note the size of the foot on this yearling.

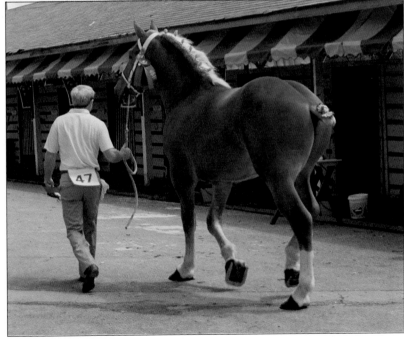

Senior Champion Stallion was Orndorff's Supreme U2, shown here with his usual enthusiasm by owner Corbly Orndorff.

Orndorff's Supreme U-2.

Five year old Jay-Lou Supreme was one of 20 breeding stallions brought to the show for exhibition in a special stallion barn, but not entered in the competition. Jay-Lou Supreme is owned by Chris Jess, and is a half brother of U2 pictured above — both are sired by Orndorff's Congolaise Supreme.

Bob Whisman showed Taylor Creek Stric-O-Luck to first in a class of forty-seven 2-year-old fillies. She then went on to be named Reserve Grand Champion Mare.

Beth Graham of Schomberg, Ontario, showed Remlap Constance Edie Johne to first in the yearling filly class and to Reserve Junior Champion Mare.

A daily Parade of Breeds at the Horse Park showcases dozens of different breeds. The Shire horse was presented as a medieval war horse.

The Country Hitch team waiting to enter the coliseum.

Draft horse and draft mule teams pull trolleys filled with visitors on a tour of the Horse Park all day, with the teams being changed every two hours.

Jesse Pareo, age 12, won both the Junior Driver Team and Junior Driver Cart classes.

Don Schneckloth showed TBM Mark to second in a strong class of fifteen 2-year-olds. Don has been showing Belgian horses since 1934!

Windmill Acres took first in the tandem class, with Joe Detweiler driving.

Dean Woodbury took first in the Driving Competition class, turning in a drive that both delighted and awed the crowd. Dean drove a series of backing maneuvers, circles, and swirls with the added handicap of the crowd's involuntary gasps of approval, making it hard for the horses to hear his instructions — but still it was a flawless drive. He left the ring accompanied by a standing ovation, making the judge's job (for first place) very easy. Each competitor in this class was free to do whatever he wished within the allocated time, making the class exciting and unpredictable. It was, for me, the highpoint of the show. Riding with Dean after the award was presented was his wife, Kelly.

A horsepull was held on both Friday and Saturday night. Here two of the pulling horses are being lunged, as a team, in the afternoon before the pull.

Windmill Acres, with Joe Detweiler driving, won both the six and four horse classes, as well as the tandem and the unicorn classes. This team certainly came into its own at Lexington, serving notice that it was the team to beat in the future.

Paul Sparrow brought one of the Coors exhibition hitches to the Championship show, putting on a demonstration drive (including this gallop across the length of the arena) each evening.

Harold McMain, here driving his team of registered mares, celebrated his 75th birthday during the show.

Jim Hilgendorf did some of the driving for the Pareo family of Veguita, New Mexico. Here he presents an exciting picture as he leaves the ring with the Pareo six. Upon exiting the ring he stopped and Todd Radermacher climbed on the seat for a ride back to the barns. It is apparent that Todd had been doing some shopping at the Mischka Farm booth — one of the many booths around the perimeter of the arena. (Sorry, I couldn't resist that.)

There's always a mane flower that needs to be straightened while you wait to go into the ring. This is the Tom Justin entry in the foreground, with Kim Sigmon adjusting a flower on the Windmill Acres entry in the background.

The Country Hitch team driven by David Helmuth, with Vikki Lynn Thompson riding. The next summer (1993) David and Vikki took the Country Hitch for a journey across the United States, and got married on that trip. See the Country Hitch story on page 64.

Horse shows usually involve a lot of waiting, and this one was no exception. At the top, in partial silhouette, is the Woodside Farm team with Dean Woodbury on the seat. At the bottom is the Harry Farr Family unicorn, Steve Gregg with the lines.

This is the 11-yr-old stallion, Orndorff's Congolaise Supreme, one of the stallions exhibited in Stallion Row, and the sire of the two stallions pictured on page 46. This stallion is one of the cornerstones of the very successful breeding program at Orndorff's Belgians of Waynesburg, Pennsylvania, named the Premier Breeder at this show.

Standing at the head of a very large and strong aged Gelding class, and going on to be named Grand Champion Gelding, was Hooch, owned by Darrell & Susan Drain of Stoney Lake Belgians in Ontario and shown by Randy Robertson. This horse went on to be Champion at all the big shows in 1993.

Each February the northern Wisconsin town of Eagle River hosts a mid-winter festival called Klondike Days, with the biggest event being the dog sled races. In 1994 they decided to add a horsepull. Several loads of sand were spread on the pavement and the teams pulled a sled loaded with logs. The mixed team at the top is owned by Maynard Siedie of Brodhead, Wisconsin. The big team at the right is owned and driven by Ben Reed of Bear Lake, Michigan. Ben is a professional horse-logger and horsepuller, and he won this event. The crowd seemed to prefer the horsepull to the dog sled races.

Horsepulling

Horsepulling, at least here in the Midwest, involves pulling a loaded sled (or Dynamometer machine) a distance of 27.5 feet. When using a sled the team must stay within a 16 foot wide path marked off with ropes. There are time limits for hooking, and each contestant has three opportunities to pull the load. Teams are eliminated when they are unable to pull the load the required distance. The team which pulls the heaviest load the farthest is the winner.

Wisconsin has a very active Horse Pullers Association, with over 500 members and a full schedule of pulls from May through October. There are often four pulls scheduled each weekend — two in the northern part of the state and two in the southern. Other Midwestern states have similar Associations.

The sport is well organized, with dozens of rules which govern individual contests. Contest winners accumulate points leading to overall high-point awards at the end of the year. Drug tests are given to the horses on a random basis to make sure that the sport is drug-free. Sportsmanship and

Dale Huston of Cottage Grove, Wisconsin, with his heavyweight team at a 1992 pull in Elkhorn, Wisconsin.

Horsemanship awards are given to encourage behaviour which will be pleasing to the spectators.

Horsepulling is a spectator sport, with large crowds gathering for most pulls. It is an activity with an objective method of determining the winner so that the spectator always understands who is winning, and why. This, plus the size and strength of the horses, makes it a very popular draft horse activity.

Luke and Colonel, a team of 7-year-old Belgian geldings owned and driven by Dennis Armitage of Cambridge, Wisconsin. This heavyweight pair has a combined weight of 5090 pounds. Here they are pulling at Waukon, Iowa.

Two scenes from the Walworth County Fair in Elkhorn, Wisconsin, where a large crowd gathers each Labor Day Monday for a horsepull. The teamsters here are all from Elkhorn. Tommy Markham is driving the top team with his dad, Kenny, encouraging him. John Osborne is driving the bottom team with his brother, Rich, worrying alongside.

A Percheron pulling horse owned by Gary Smith of North Freedom, Wisconsin.

This team belongs to Leonard Tostenson of Houston, Minnesota — a loud exception to the general rule that most pulling horses are Belgians.

A handsome team belonging to Todd Sowles of Beloit, Wisconsin, at a pull in Palmyra, Wisconsin.

A horsepull consists of short bursts of power and energy separated by long periods of rest and contemplation. This is Alan Grass of Blair, Wisconsin, with his team called Duke and Bob. This pair of 7- and 8-year-old geldings have a combined weight of 3,600 pounds.

This is Al Waletzko (Arcadia, Wisconsin) and his heavyweight team, Sandy and Barney. These horses are calm while waiting to pull, but all business when they are hooked to the sled. This team has a combined weight of 4,600 pounds.

Virgil Perry of Spring Valley, Wisconsin, and his team of Jim and Jerry do sleigh rides in the winter months. This team was the highpoint heavyweight pulling team for the State of Wisconsin in 1992.

A heavyweight team owned and driven by Dale Huston of Cottage Grove, Wisconsin at a 1993 pull in Elkhorn, Wisconsin. This team went on to win first at the Detroit International over 31 other teams, pulling 4,400 pounds on a dynamometer a distance of 19 feet.

Country's Reminisce Hitch comes into small town America, loaded with people who made reservations to take part in this historic adventure.

The Hitch began it's trip with a romp in the Atlantic Ocean, and started the second half of the trip with a similar romp on the Pacific. This photo of the Atlantic splash was mounted on the side of their motorhome. It made a nice photo, but the salt water was not good for the harness.

Country's Reminisce Hitch

One of the biggest draft horse stories in 1993/94, and surely the longest-lasting one, was the six horse Belgian hitch which walked across the entire length of the United States, from Maine to California.

Roy Reiman is a publisher of magazines aimed at the rural market. He started in 1986 with a magazine called *Country* — which now has 2.5 million loyal, enthusiastic, almost fanatic subscribers. Other magazines were added, including *Reminisce, Taste of Home, Farm & Ranch Living, Country Handcrafts*, and *Country Woman*. A mail-order gift business, world-wide tours, and book publishing round out this growing and evolving enterprise.

Roy has had a long interest in draft horses. He was involved in the first 40 horse hitch put together by Dick Sparrow, and purchased several of those horses when the 40 was disbanded. He sponsored the Belgian show hitch of Brookside Farms in 1992, calling it the Country Hitch. I personally noticed many of Roy's subscribers attending draft horse shows in 1992 *just because the Country Hitch was there.*

At the end of the 1992 show year Roy purchased the Brookside horses and announced that in 1993 they would undertake a cross-country trip, from Maine to California, to visit the subscribers of his magazines. The hitch was to be called Country's Reminisce Hitch, bringing together the names of two of his most popular magazines. The teamster would be David Helmuth, the young man who had already been showing and travelling with these horses for the past two years.

What an exciting and ambitious project! They started out in the Atlantic Ocean off the coast of Maine on April 13, 1993. By October 23 they had reached Centerville, Iowa, and the weather was getting too cold to continue. It was just too big an undertaking to complete in one year.

After a truck ride to San Diego and a short rest period the hitch started out again from the Pacific Ocean on December 13th, this time travelling east. On August 12th, 1994, they arrived back in Centerville, Iowa, thereby completing their cross-country walk. Over 5,000 people came out to celebrate the completion of this epic adventure.

I spent a day watching the Country Reminisce Hitch on September 29, 1993, in and between the towns of Forrest and Fairbury, Illinois. It was easy to get caught up in the excitement, and I did.

David Helmuth and Vikki Thompson have become bigger than life, like rock stars or football heroes, to the subscribers of the Reiman magazines. They were married on August 14, 1993, near Sugarcreek, Ohio, as 5,000 subscribers from 22 states and Canada looked on. This almost life-size image of the couple appears on the back of the van which travels with the hitch, and which is their home during this adventure.

The arrival of the Country's Reminisce Hitch in your town is a big event. Just imagine, they are walking clear across the country, and will be stopping in our town! Here the Prairie Central High School Band welcomes the Hitch as they approach the downtown area of Fairbury, Illinois. This is small town mid-America in all its glory.

David Helmuth

The first stop in Fairbury was the Hospital. Dave drove the team down a congested street and under the canopy in front of the hospital entrance. After walking down streets and highways for 10 miles each day for the past six months these horses are really broke, and Dave handles them beautifully. Dave gave a short talk to the hospital staff and patients at the hospital entrance, explaining their trip, and then drove on toward the Fairview Haven Nursing Home.

David guides the hitch into the front driveway of the Fairview Haven Nursing Home. The lettering on the side of the hitchwagon says "We are Pulling for Seniors!", and the arrival of the hitch is surely a high point in these senior citizen's lives. The passengers in the back of the wagon are residents of the Nursing Home that were loaded up for a ride when the hitch came into town.

Then it was on to the next stop, with many more miles of travel and people to meet before the end of the day. Early in the trip the harness was modified to replace the normal scotch collars with the breast collar arrangement you see here. The show-type scotch collars are rather stiff, and do not fit as well as the normal work collars. These breast collars are much cooler and and lighter, and more comfortable on the horses.

Early in the afternoon the hitch stops for the day, and the horses go into these portable stalls set up under a tent alongside the semi-trailer. The people come to see the horses in their stalls and buy souvenirs of the trip.

Both the old and the young, and those in-between, marvelled at these big horses. This was a real "hands-on" experience for the public.

This is the other side of the semi-trailer as it is parked for the night, with people posing for pictures in front of the painting on the trailer.

Subscribers of the Reiman magazines were invited to take a ride in the back of the wagon for a part of the trip. They were loaded (and unloaded) at rural crossroads and at scheduled stops in the cities. Here one group of passengers is getting off, and another group is waiting to get on, just west of Fairbury on highway 24. At the halfway point of the trip (at the end of 1993) over 13,000 people had ridden in the back of the wagon as passengers.

And then it was off to the next stop in Forrest, Illinois. The right wheeler in the hitch is Bobby, the 1992 Grand Champion Gelding at the National Belgian Show (page 100). The left wheeler is only a three-year-old who was broke on the trip. These are all quality horses who would do well in any showring.

The arena for the Live Oak Invitational is open on three sides, with one solid wall on the West side. There are bleachers on three sides, and vendors have booths against the solid wall. This is Alan Freitag driving the Live Oak Plantation tandem entry.

This is the Pennwoods four of Percherons, with Chad Cole driving and John Cole riding.

1993 Live Oak Invitational

Ocala, Florida, can be a delightful place in February, especially to those of us who live the the northern part of the U.S. It was in 1993. The 1993 Live Oak Invitational show was blessed with warm temperatures and sunny skies as it hosted the finals for the 1992 North American Six-Horse Hitch Classic Series (hereafter called the "Classic").

The Classic competition began in 1989 to encourage the showing of six-horse hitches and increase the public's awareness of this phase of draft horse showing. Competitors earn points during the year by placing at 68 different shows throughout the United States and Canada, with the top twelve hitches (four from each breed — Clydes and Shires are lumped together) meeting at a final competition to determine the overall annual champion. For the 1992 Classic this final competition was held at the 1993 Live Oak Invitational.

A total of 217 six-horse hitches entered the 1992 Classic competition, and 10 of the top 12 attended the finals in Ocala. After the dust settled the Windmill Acres six of Belgians was crowned the 1992 Classic Champion — for the third consecutive year!

The Windmill Acres six leaves the ring after being named the Six-Horse Champion of this Show. The driver is Joe Detweiler. Riding with Joe is Tom Penhale who donated and presented the handsome trophy. Tom builds very fine hitch wagons in his shop near Bayfield, Ontario.

Dr. and Mrs. John C. Weber (of Ocala) started the Live Oak Invitational in 1989, and continue to be its prime mover. It is a hitch competition only (no halter classes), with the classes spread over five afternoons. The showgrounds are the Ocala Arabian Breeders Show Grounds, and the classes take place in a covered arena open on three sides. Large crowds attend this show including many northerners who come for a brief respite from winter. Yes, central Florida can be delightful in early February.

Jaqui Westbrook, age 14, gets ready to enter the ring in the Junior Driver class with a team from the Live Oak Plantation. With Jaqui is her father, Jim Westbrook, trainer for the Live Oak Plantation. This team had been in the previous class, and their feather has lost a little of its brightness (see page 76).

Bob Robinson brought the Clydes into the ring with music from his bag pipes.

Another entry in the Junior Driver class was David Schumacher shown here leaving the ring after placing second in a tough class of 14. With David is his father, Harold Schumacher, owner of the team of Percheron geldings.

Carl Moulton drives his Shire six, the only Shire team at the show, into the staging area. Mr. Moulton's farm is called the New England Shire Centre, and is located in Lebanon, New Hampshire.

Dr. Eugene Hussey also took the long drive from New Hampshire to take part in this show. Dr. Hussey is a veterinarian in North Conway whose favorite recreation is driving his grey Percherons. Alongside Dr. Hussey is Don Langille.

The Windmill Acres six was named 1992 North American Classic Series Champion at this show, the third consecutive year they have achieved this honor! The driver is Joe Detweiler and his assistant is the farm manager, Kim Sigmon.

Edd Sigmon, owner of
Windmill Acres Farm,
Newton, North Carolina.

The beautifully turned out six from Live Oak Plantation with Jim Westbrook driving.

This is Dr. John C. Weber. Mr. & Mrs. Weber are the host of the Live Oak Invitational and owners of the Live Oak Plantation.

A Stoney Lake Belgians team.

The unicorn team of the Siftons, with Don McNeil driving and Dr. Dennis Sifton riding.

This is Tom Justin's four-abreast team. This was prior to the class, and their overchecks are still loose.

Warren Torgerson with his team of Percheron Geldings makes a pretty picture as he enters the ring. Warren came from his home near Clearbrook, Minnesota, probably the farthest distance that any exhibitor travelled to get to Ocala.

Scott Banga brings the tandem entry owned by Bill Dean of Waverly, Iowa, out of the ring at a brisk trot.

Sterling Farms won the Supreme Champion eight over all breeds at the 1993 Live Oak Invitational, with Darrel Madson driving assisted by his son-in-law, Dean Woodbury.

Darrel and Dean leaving the ring with the trophy donated by Dr. and Mrs. John C. Weber.

Avery Sterling, Jr. of Gladwin, Michigan, owner of the Sterling Farm hitch.

The Harry Farr & Family entry, with Steve Gregg driving and his wife, Beth Gregg, assisting.

The Harold Schumacher entry, with Harold driving and Rick Riemer assisting.

*The McKenzie Clydesdale entry,
with Edgar Hughes driving.*

*Pennwoods Percherons, with Chad Cole
driving and his father, John Cole, assisting.*

It's a relatively short drive from Ocala to Orlando where you will find the Magic Kingdom in Walt Disney World. Here a trolley drawn by a Belgian horse waits in front of Cinderalla's Castle for some passengers.

I love to take pictures of seagulls. On this picture the six-horse Disney hitch of Percherons was about to make the gull forget about his lunch, at least temporarily. The seagulls are very aggressive at Disney World. One took a bite out of my ice cream cone as I was walking down the sidewalk.

A Percheron gelding pulls a trolley along Main Street at the Disney Magic Kingdom theme park. Neither these horses or the six horse hitch wear the diapers which are mandatory at most city street carriage ride operations. I guess there are sufficient employees around to pick up the manure as necessary. The horse's name is Dan, and the driver is Bill Carr.

The wheelers are hooked, and waiting for the others to be brushed, harnessed, and hooked.

Are these legs clean, or what?

Mike waits in the trailer until the horses are harnessed and hitched; then he comes out and checks things over before taking his place on the wagon seat.

Budweiser Clydes

Their official name is The World Famous Budweiser Clydesdales, but we know them as the Budweiser Clydes. They are, without question, the most famous draft horses of all time.

The story is well known. Formally introduced to August Busch, Sr. on April 7, 1933 by his son, August Busch, Jr., the Budweiser Clydes have become goodwill ambassadors for both the Anheuser-Busch company and the entire draft horse world. To many people, perhaps most people, all draft horses are Budweiser horses.

There are now three travelling hitches, making a total of over 300 appearances each year, and travelling 90,000 miles in the process. The hitches are based in St. Louis, Romoland (California), and Merrimack (New Hampshire). In addition there are Budweiser Clydes on display at the breweries in St. Louis, Merrimack, and Fort Collins (Colorado) and at theme parks owned by Anheuser-Busch in Florida, Virginia, Texas, and California.

The Budweiser Clydes are truly the "cream of the crop" in the Clydesdale world. Their geldings are both correct and massive, as are their breeding horses. Hitch geldings must be at least 3 years of age, 18 hands tall, bay with four white stockings and a white blaze, and weigh between 1,800 and 2,300 pounds. The search for these animals, both in North America and Scotland, is never ending.

The Budweiser Clydes make appearances when asked to by the local beer distributor. The distributor, in turn, takes care of the local advertising. If the Clydes are coming to your town or area you will know it, for the distributor will have billboards and posters up and will run stories in the local papers.

At this appearance the horses were housed in a local Armory. Their (two) appearances were each scheduled for the afternoon, and the public was invited to come see them in their stalls each morning.

I spent a couple of days with the St. Louis hitch as it made appearances in Northern Wisconsin and Upper Michigan. I was impressed with the animals, and with their crew. This is *show business*, surely. But, as with much of show business, there was lots of hard work and patience with precious little glamour and excitement. The crew I watched handled the boredom and endless, repetititve questions from the crowd with grace and dignity.

With three hitches constantly on the road you'd think we would run into these horses from time to time. Not so. This is a big country. Until I tracked them down and made a point to see them I had never seen them except for the Milwaukee Circus Parade. But if you do have the opportunity to see them I urge you to take it. The Budweiser Clydes are a class act — goodwill ambassadors for the entire draft horse industry.

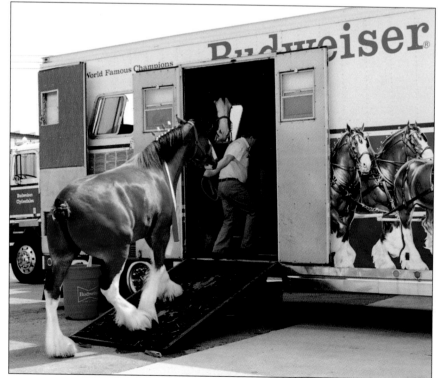

After a morning of bathing, brushing, and braiding eight of the ten horses that travel with each hitch (two are spares) are loaded into two especially built 40' semi-trailers. Each trailer is equipped with a television camera system so that the driver can keep an eye on the horses. A third semi-trailer hauls the hitch wagon and harness.

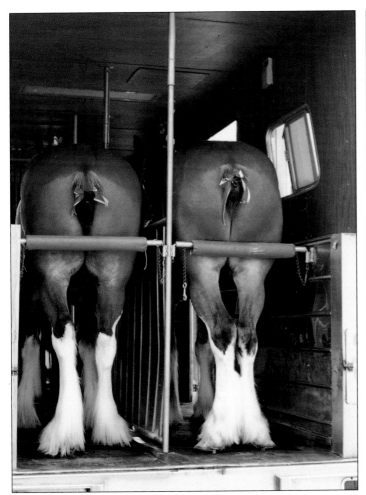

During loading the back doors of the trailer were opened for ventilation. The trailers were so clean they looked as though they had never seen a horse before. And look at those fetlocks!

This is what it's all about — the wonder of a child. (And selling some beer to her parents.)

This was a shopping center appearance, and the trucks arrived well in advance of the advertised time (and the crowds). The doors on the horse trailers are opened for ventilation, and the hitch wagon is about to be unloaded.

For this shopping center appearance the unloading, polishing...

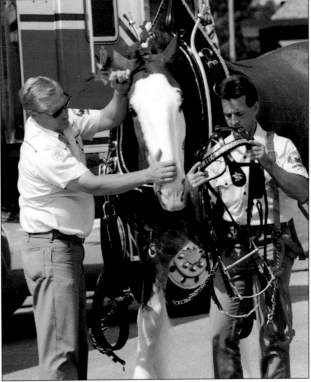

harnessing, and hooking up was all part of the show, done out in the open for the crowd to enjoy.

The World Famous Budweiser Clydesdales, with Jim Hilgendorf doing the driving, Dan Wright as assistant driver, Mickey as official dalmatian.

Driver Jim Hilgendorf poses for photos with the local Budweiser distributor, Dennis Bovin.

The next day Assistant Driver Alan Schneckloth was on the box with Jim Hilgendorf. Each man in the crew gets one day off each week, on a rotating basis, since the hitch makes appearances seven days a week. Tony Pichler was the out-walker.

When doing an appearance, as opposed to a parade, the hitch may stand in place for an hour or more while the crowd asks questions and takes pictures. The drivers have to be very patient as the crowd turns over and new people ask the same questions. Here Jim, Mickey, and Alan are enjoying the crowd.

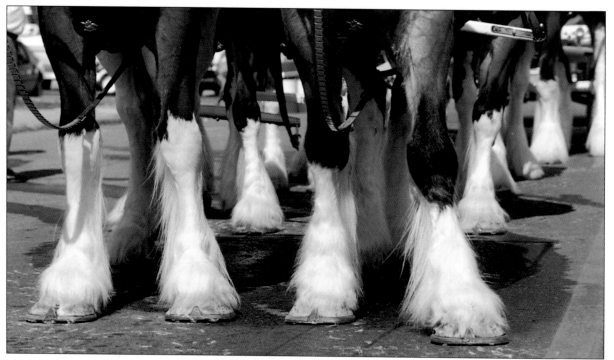

These are clean, well-shod feet. Anyone who has ever shod a draft horse, or washed a Clyde or Shire, will appreciate the work that is involved in keeping feet like this.

At the end of the scheduled appearance the horses are unhooked, unharnessed, and re-loaded into their trailer. When the front six horses are unhooked Jim and the wheel team take the wagon to the end of the trailer in which it is hauled — then these horses are also unhooked.

Then it's on the road again.

These two photos were taken during the Wisconsin State Fair in Milwaukee during August, 1993. The top photo the team is beginning to be hitched for their nightly exhibition drive in the arena, with the usual crowd of bystanders watching. The wet spots on the pavement are from the leg-washing of the geldings which was just completed. The bottom photo is of the hitch doing their exhibition drive before a packed house in the arena.

In the book Draft Horses Today *I expressed some concern about the future of the Budweiser Clydesdales following the death of August Busch, Jr. Not to worry. The Anheuser-Busch Company has gotten into the entertainment business in a big way, and are using their Clydesdales as an integral part of that business. These two photos were taken at Sea World in Orlando, Florida, now owned by Anheuser-Busch. There is a hitch at other theme parks in San Diego, Tampa, Williamsburg (Virginia), as well as individual horses at San Antonio and Fort Collins (Colorado).*

This is the Harry Farr & Family entry, from Dunnville, Ontario, at the 1992 National Belgian Show in Davenport, Iowa. The four is being driven by Steve Gregg.

1992 National Belgian Show

The first of the national breed shows to take place each summer is the National Belgian Show. It is held as part of the Mississippi Valley Fair in Davenport, Iowa, usually the first week-end of August. The Mississippi Valley Fair is an old-fashioned midwestern county fair, with a healthy emphasis on farm animals and exhibits. Having said this, however, I am confident that the Belgian Show is one of the main attractions at this Fair.

In 1992, the year we attended, the Belgian community was gearing up for the Belgian Championship II Show in Lexington in September. This took a little of the prestige off the National Show. Despite this a total of 38 exhibitors from throughout the United States and Canada brought a good turnout of horses to Davenport in August.

The halter classes are held on Thursday inside a metal building. There is some seating inside the building, with the crowd also filling the open doorways at both ends and one side of the building. The hitch classes are held in an outdoor arena at the South end of the fairgrounds, with the classes spread over Friday evening, Saturday evening, and Sunday afternoon. There is a small covered grandstand on one side of the outdoor arena, with many spectators on their lawn chairs surrounding the arena fence. On Sunday afternooon a second outdoor arena is used for draft farm team classes.

It's refreshing to be able to see some of the best Belgians in the country — the same horses that will be winning at the State Fairs and at Detroit later in the year — in a relaxed, uncrowded county fair atmosphere. No long walks from the parking lot, no large crowds, no hassle.

The Main Entrance Gate to the Mississippi Valley Fair.

David Helmuth shows Bobby to Grand Champion Gelding honors for the "Country Hitch", a hitch owned by Brookside Farm in Stockton, California, and leased to Roy Reiman Publications for the 1992 season. Reiman publishes Country Magazine (among others), which is where the name Country Hitch came from. At the left of the picture in the white shirt is Maurice Telleen, publisher of the Draft Horse Journal.

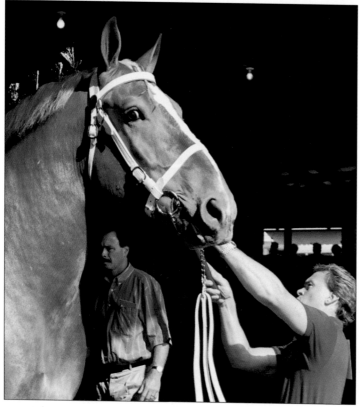

Another Country Hitch gelding being examined by the judge, John Beattie, of Stayner, Ontario.

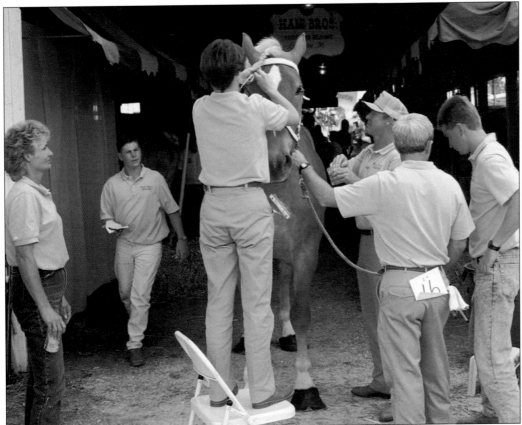

The Hale Brothers (Gary and Jack) are consistent winners at halter. At this show they won the Breeders Award, each of the group classes, Grand Champion Stallion, and Reserve Champion Mare. They start with good horses and are among the best in conditioning, fitting, and showing. And it doesn't hurt to have 6 people who know what to do get your horses ready to go into the showring. Jack is holding the horse, and Gary is wearing the cap.

The four-abreast halter entry of Harry Farr, Dunnville, Ontario.

The Country Hitch to[o] first in t[he] four-abreast halter class.

Bob Johnson of Delmar, Iowa, gave a thrilling exhibition ride with his six of Appaloosas hitched to a stagecoach. Riding with Bob is Don Schneckloth who was honored for his past efforts on behalf of the National Show.

The Country Hitch took first in both the four and six horse hitch classes. Riding with David Helmuth is Phyllis Grupe who, with her husband, Fritz, own the horses in this hitch. This team was leased to Reiman Publications (Country magazine) for 1992. See the Country Hitch story on page 65.

*Craig Grange with Cody,
his Reserve Grand
Champion Gelding.*

*Krista Grange, age 7, held the
lines for her father's hitch as
horses were added or changed
between classes.*

*The team of mares entry of Bill and Judy Crouch. The parasol
probably started out to be part of Judy's costume but it ended up
almost essential as the temperature soared into the high 90s.*

*Darrel Eberspacher showed the
Reserve Grand Champion Stallion,
Greentop Cody.*

Elroy Brass has been showing Belgian horses since 1950. He has slowed some, but is still a fierce competitor.

A Woodside Farm gelding and his decorated bridle.

Chris Schwarck took a second with his team of mares.

Marc Gravert showed his team in the farm classes that ran in a different arena on Sunday. The judge alternated between the show arena and the farm class arena, as did some of the spectators.

Windmill Acres, Joe Detweiler driving, John Sigmon riding.

Craig Grange, with daughter Krista.

Harold McMain

Dean Woodbury with the Woodside Farm entry.

This is the Bill Hauser bandwagon, being pulled by their six Belgians. The 5 ton wagon was built on the Hauser farm in Mindoro, Wisconsin, with Bill's son, Chuck, doing most of the work. This hitch is a regular feature at the Waukon parade.

One of the 40 horse hitch horses, with another close behind.

Jean Schreiber of Plainview, Minnesota, took the lines from her husband, Merle, on the way back to the Sweeney farm.

1993 Waukon Parade

Ray Sweeney is an auctioneer who lives in Waukon, Iowa. Late each summer he hosts a Waukon Threshing Days celebration, which includes a horsepull, threshing and plowing demonstrations, crafts, and a large parade. The parade is always several hours long, with over a hundred horse drawn units. It is the only parade I know of where the participants can see the parade, and the spectators can see it twice without moving, for the parade route is down Waukon's main street, and then back up the same street to where it started. It's a wide street, and the parade units pass each other as they come back to the starting area.

For many years Ray had been asking his friend, Dick Sparrow, to bring the 40 horse hitch to his parade. As you can imagine, assembling the 40 is a major undertaking. It has been many years since the 40 has appeared anywhere but at the Milwaukee Circus Parade. But after many years of being asked, and saying "no", Dick finally said "Alright, we'll come, but this is what it will cost." Ray gasped when he heard the number, but then said OK. It may never happen again, but this is how a parade in a little town in Northeast Iowa landed the 40 horse hitch for their 1993 parade — all through the generosity of Ray Sweeney.

The 1993 Waukon Threshing Days Parade didn't start on time. This picture was taken a half hour after the parade was to have started, but there were still hundreds of spectators walking to the parade route after parking their cars up to a mile away. The 40 horse hitch is quite an attraction.

This is Kevin Barth from the nearby town of Decorah getting acquainted with one of the 40 horse hitch Belgians.

Ray Sweeney playing the drums in a band while riding a wagon in the parade

Just a part of the 40 horse hitch horses tied on a picket line before being harnessed for the parade.

The top photo shows the 40 horse hitch turning the corner, coming onto the parade route, with the wagon (and Dick Sparrow, the driver), to the left of the picture, still on the side street. At the bottom the 40 is moving down the main street of Waukon, with the spectators watching. A single horse in a cart is moving away from the camera, back to the starting place of the parade.

Old Time Logging

Each year the Carriage Association of America (CAA) holds two conferences for its members, a large doings each spring at a prominent location such as the Biltmore Estate in Ashville, North Carolina, or the Kentucky Horse Park in Lexington, Kentucky, and then a smaller affair in the winter, usually in a warm, sunny location. In 1992 the CAA departed from their normal warm location for the winter conference, accepting an invitation from the Minnesota Wheels and Whips driving club to have it in St. Paul, Minnesota, in conjunc-

Dave Schubert and his four Percherons move the large logging bobsled loaded with logs. The sled runners are 8' apart, and the sled platform is 12' wide. The track for the sled runners are iced, and the horses walk in the un-iced area between the runners. Extra "snatch" teams are hooked to the sled corners to help it start moving, as the moving runners generate heat which causes the sled to freeze tight whenever it is stopped for loading. The logs on this load weigh about 36,000 pounds.

Positioning the log on the sled as it is lowered by a cable looped over the log jammer. Another team of horses pulls the cable, lifting the logs up onto the sled.

tion with the St. Paul Winter Carnival. One of the main features of the Conference, in addition to the normal seminars and clinics, was the Sleigh and Cutter Parade hosted by the St. Croix (Wisconsin) Driving Club as part of the Carnival each year.

When Thomas Boelz of Clear Lake, Minnesota, heard about these plans he volunteered to organize an old-time logging demonstration for the benefit of the CAA members and St. Paul Carnival attendees. Similar demonstrations had been held each year in Bemidji, Minnesota, sponsored by the local lumberyard. For the one in St. Paul Tom would make it even more special by building some new horse-drawn equipment — a snow roller, and a huge bobsled.

Snow rollers were used before the days of automobiles to pack down the snow on the roadways so that the horse-drawn sleighs could travel more easily. Tom had seen pictures of the old snow rollers, and made a new one from the pictures, painting it a bright red.

The bobsled Tom built was a replica of one that had been used to carry 50 passengers from the train station to the hotels in Duluth, Minnesota, at the turn of the Century. It was 28 feet long and required 6 horses to pull it on the snow-packed streets. Tom had seen a picture of the sleigh in his copy of *Heroes in Harness*, a book of old photographs by Philip Weber, and built his replica by looking at that photo, without any drawings.

Dave Schubert of Brainerd, Minnesota, brought some of his Percheron horses to skid logs, operate the log jammer, and pull the large logging bobsled. Dave had demonstrated these activities at the previous logging demonstrations in Bemidji, and he and his horses knew their jobs very well. Dave Stalheim brought some of his Clydesdales to pull the snow roller, Gerald Foust brought his Clydes to pull the new bobsled, and other draft horse people brought their horses to fill out the activities.

The weather was beautiful — too warm for the Carnival Ice Palace which melted in the warm sun and had to be humanely destroyed before the end of the Carnival weekend — but very nice for the thousands of spectators who came to see how logging was done "in the old days".

Dave Stalheim driving four of his Clydesdales, pulling the snow roller built by Tom Boelz. With Dave is Bob Bjorndahl and Dave's son, Andrew.

Another shot of Dave and his Clydes pulling the snow roller. With Dave on his far right is Tom Boelz. On his left is Steve Olson, a CAA Director from California.

Tom Boelz

Justin (driving the horses) and Andrew (with lines) Stalheim drive a team of their father's Clydes out to be hooked on the snow roller. These are lead lines for an eight, so Andrew has his hands·full.

Four Clydesdales owned and driven by Gerald Foust pull the 50 passenger bobsled. Later in the day, as the crowds grew in number and the load got heavier, he hitched six to the sled — and all six were needed.

Dr. Charles Mayo brought his team of Belgians, Arla and Maggie, adding to the festivities by pulling a small bobsled loaded with firewood.

There was a sleigh ralley in a nearby park — another part of the St. Paul Winter Carnival. At the top we see C. J. and Geri Aune of Cannon Falls, Minnesota, driving a pair of Percherons hooked to a fancy cutter. At the bottom Janet Voeltz of Jefferson, Wisconsin, drives her team of Norwegian Fjord ponies to an equally fancy sleigh.

Nevada City Carriage Co.

Nevada City, California, sits at the foothills of the High Sierras, a couple of hours drive east from Sacramento, at an altitude of 2,500 feet. It is the Seat of Nevada County whose mines have yielded more than half of California's total production of gold. After a freeway came through and demolished many of the town's historic buildings the city fathers decided that those (buildings) which remained should be protected and preserved for reasons both cultural and economic. The town of 2,900 people is now one big historic district which attracts thousands of tourists to the many specialty shops located in the downtown area. It is here that David Vertin operates the Nevada City Carriage Co.

One of the bright blue Nevada City Carriage Co. carriages in front of the National Hotel, waiting for a fare. The horse is a Percheron gelding called Jerry.

Jeramy Johnson tells her passengers the history of the house they are passing, as the Percheron gelding, Jerry, makes another of his very frequent trips up this hill.

David's Nevada City Carriage Company gives horse-drawn rides through the historic districts of the city, using Percheron horses pulling blue carriages driven by knowledgeable lady drivers. The lady drivers are well-versed in the history of the area, and they do a wonderful job of passing this knowledge on to their passengers. The normal tour costs $10 for two people, and it lasts about an hour. Additional passengers cost $2 each. Longer or specific tours can be arranged. Picnic and other specialty tours are being planned for the future.

The carriages and carriage horses are housed in a turn of the century carriage house which David was building when we visited him in the spring of 1993. The lumber used to build the carriage house (and there was a lot of it) was logged and sawed by David as part of another of his businesses, the Cedar Creek Horselogging & Milling Co.

David's Cedar Creek operation involves the purchase of standing timber, cutting down the trees, skidding the fallen trees with Percheron horses to his portable sawmill, sawing the logs into boards, air-drying the lumber, and finally milling the lumber into finished sizes and shapes. This is much easier said than done. We watched him skid some cedar trees out of the brush to his portable sawmill and were impressed by how hard the work was, both for Dave and for his horses. We were impressed with the way in which his logging horses trusted him, walking into dense brush and tight situations that demanded their complete confidence.

Another part of the Cedar Creek operation is the Cedar Creek Hitch-wagon Co. Here Dave builds a new 5th wheel running gear with wooden wheels and 2" roller bearing axles for hitch wagons or other wagons which require a 5th wheel turntable.

It is already apparent that David Vertin is one busy fellow. But that's not all. Dave has a herd of 25-30 registered Percheron horses, including foaling mares and a stallion at stud. He has a large vegetable garden and cans the excess produce for the winter. He raises the hay needed by his horses, and the horses help put it up. Dave helped found the Carriage Operators of America, and currently serves as it's President. Rubber-cushioned horseshoes for carriage horses are another interest of his, and he wholesales and distributes a new shoe of this type. And I'm sure this is just a partial list of his activities and enthusiasms, as we only spent part of two days with him.

Nevada City has installed genuine gas lamps in their downtwon area, the only other town besides New Orleans to do so.

The entrance to the new Carriage Barn (under construction) which will be the headquarters for the Nevada City Carriage Co. David not only designed and constructed the building himself (with the aid of a couple of carpenters and a mason), but he also cut, dried, and sawed the wood which was used to frame and enclose the building. This is a massive building (100' x 40') constructed the way someone with money and pride might have done it at the turn of the 20th century.

Jeramy gives Mary Mischka a tour of Nevada City, using David's 12 year old stallion, Joe. It is a little unusual to use a stallion for carriage work, especially one that is also used for breeding, but Joe has been doing this work for many years and is quite good at it.

A view of the Carriage Barn from the highway. The lower floor contains horse stalls and a carriage storage area. Offices and an apartment for the carriage manager are upstairs.

On the busy weekends Dave takes a turn driving carriage. Here he is with Jerry, framed by the gaslights.

Not a part of Dave's operation, but part of Nevada City, is this planned sculpture of a draft horse skidding a sled of logs. This monumental piece (18' tall x 44' long) will be cast in bronze and placed at the entrance of the Nevada City Fairgrounds as soon as the necessary funds are raised. Pictured here is the artist, Todd Andrews, with his full-size clay model of the sculpture.

Dave Vertin leaves his portable sawmill with his logging team, chainsaw on his shoulder, to skid some logs to the landing.

Dave brings the first cedar log up to the landing. This was a long, heavy log, and the team had to bring it up a relatively steep incline. It isn't always possible to set up the site so the landing is downhill from the logs. Being the first log of the session neither the horses or Dave show any signs of sweat — this will change.

Dave jumps over the load as the team pulls two smaller logs up the path, toward the sawmill.

Dave and his team bring another cedar log to the landing. At this point, after locating and skidding about 10 logs, both the team and Dave are sweating. This is hard, dangerous work, both for the team and for the teamster.

The Iowa-Minnesota Draft Horse Association comes together several times each year to work a field on the campus of Luther College in Decorah, Iowa. It was a cold, raw early-April day when Bob Pietan brought his team of Belgians to drill oats, but much nicer in mid-July when he came back with three horses to help bind the mature grain. Bob is from Elma, Iowa.

Work and Field Days

Each spring and fall, from one end of America to the other, draft horse folks get an itch to go out and do some field work with their horses — to go to a work or field day. Most of these events are scheduled the same time each year, on a regular basis, by local clubs and state associations. They often involve a food tent which can be a source of funds for the club or association.

When the public is invited to a work or field day it becomes a draft horse show, just as much as the shows which take place at the county fairs and state fairs each summer and fall. Some participants at work and field days may also show their horses at fairs, or at horsepulls — but for the most part the horses at a work or field day stay home the rest of the year. This is their show, and the fields are their showgrounds.

Some field days are contests, such as the plowing contests held in Minnesota each year. There the participants compete to see who can do the best job of plowing, with separate classes for walking plows and various categories of riding plows.

It is tempting to make the observation that it is only through these events the the skills involved in horse-farming are kept alive and passed on to others, but that would ignore the many Amish and others who do all their farming with horses. These skills are not disappearing; they are just becoming (much) less common.

Field and work days are public demonstrations of how people can use draft horses, giving people with these skills an opportunity to demonstrate their skills. They also offer "old-timers" a great time as they watch and reminisce, and show their grand-children how farming was once done with horses

A team of Belgians owned by Mike Baeten of De Pere, Wisconsin, stands patiently as Mike loads the wagon with oat bundles at a Farm Days hosted by the Heritage Hill Living History Museum in Green Bay, Wisconsin. Holding the lines is Roger Deviley. The steam engine and threshing machine can be seen cranking up in the background.

Judson Schrick of Decorah, Iowa, gave a good (no hands) demonstration of how a walking plow should work when it is set correctly at the Waukon (Iowa) Threshing Days celebration. Judson's horses are Flossie (on Judson's left), a registered Belgian mare and Duke, a Belgian gelding.

Two views of the threshing done at the Frontier Farming Association (NE Wisconsin) Threshing Days held at Jack Gilson's farm near Greenleaf, Wisconsin. Framing the team in the top picture we see the grain wagon used to collect the threshed oats on the right and the piping for the straw on the left. The straw was blown into a chopper (silo-filler) and then re-blown into a forage wagon, rather than making a straw-pile. The chopped straw was later blown into the Gilson barn. The picture at the right shows the lady Director and the Cameraman from the local TV station who were on hand to film the festivities.

Mike Gildernick brought three Percherons and hooked them to a sulky plow at the Frontier Farming Thresheree. Mike and his wife, Denise, live in De Pere, Wisconsin. Denise comes by her attraction to Percherons honestly as her father, Jim Kruger, is a Percheron horse-farmer in Aurora, Iowa.

A team owned and driven by Edie Robenhorst.

One problem with a Field Day, especially those in the fall which involve harvesting, is that the crop may not be ready on the day of the event. This hay was a bit sparse as Donald Vandewettering demonstrated mowing with Jack Gilson's team.

133

Peter Larsen brought a big team and demonstrated corn binding, although here again the crop was not quite ready. Peter Larsen is from Denmark, Wisconsin. He takes these big horses to "farmer's horsepulls" where the teams are unshod or wear shoes without caulks.

Ron Schaffner of Baldwin, Wisconsin, brought this lovely team to the fall Field Day sponsored by the Wisconsin Draft Horse and Mule Association. Above we see Ron driving the team, Ronnie and Rusty, pulling a wagon full of visitors at the Field Day. Later in the day this team did some discing, with Rich Anderson on the lines.

Andrew Stalheim demonstrates the use of an Imperial two-bottom walking plow at a Field Day. The plow is equipped with two steel wheels and two 10" plowshares. The horses are owned by Andrew's dad, David Stalheim, of Amery, Wisconsin. David makes a point to bring something a little bit different to the Field Days he attends.

The Fall Field Day for the Wisconsin Draft Horse and Mule Association was held at the Herman Heinbuck farm near Hammond, Wisconsin. There the straw was blown into a pile by the Oliver Red River Special, and the kids were invited to play on the pile before it was baled up. There is nothing quite so potent as a smell to bring back memories. I urge any of you who can remember threshing to attend a thresheree and smell the straw and chaff as it is blown into a pile — it will choke you up in more ways than one.

Bud Rud uses a hitch of three abreast (all mares) to pull the corn binder. Bud has nine Belgians on his farm near River Falls, Wisconsin.

Judson Schrick of Decorah, Iowa, is binding oats at the Luther College campus with his John Deere binder pulled by his four Belgians.

Walt Becker of Hillsdale, Wisconsin brings his four grey Percheron geldings and his two-bottom Huntsmen plow to most of the Field Days sponsored by the Wisconsin Association (his wife, Loretta, is Secretary of the organization). The spectators (and I) never tire of watching Walt and his team plow — they work like a well-oiled machine.

Don Parker of Webster, Wisconsin, and his six big black Percherons made an impressive sight as they plowed with a two-bottom sulky plow at the spring Field Day sponsored by the Wisconsin Association.

Bud Rud plowing at the spring Field Day using a stallion (right hand horse) and his 9-yr-old daughter hooked to a sulky plow.

These Norwegian Fjord Ponies may not be draft horses, but they sure did their share of work at the Field Day. They are owned and driven by Kate Stout of Prairie Farm, Wisconsin. Kate works them every day on her 25 acre farm. The mare walking in the furrow was due to foal about 10 days after this picture was taken.

Gail Deets

Most Field Days are sponsored by a draft horse club or organization, and are held at the farm of a member of that club or organization. But in Northern Illinois, in the town of Milledgeville, there is an Old Fashioned Horse Farming Day held each year on a late September Sunday on the Gail Deets farm.

Gail is a retired dairyfarmer who still enjoys doing some of his crop farming with horses, and is devoted to showing others how horsefarming is, and can still be, done. Gail organizes the entire event, with the help of several friends and neighbors. He makes a determined effort to show as many horsedrawn activities as possible. In addition to the traditional plowing, discing, harrowing, mowing, raking, and hayloading activities common with a fall field day he often includes grain drilling, corn binding, corn grinding, and various machines (elevators, huskers, shellers, threshers) operated by a circle horse-power.

The next six pages of photos were taken at Gail Deets' Old Fashioned Horse Farming Days.

Denver Traum brought six head of Belgians — a stallion, some geldings, and some mares — and did some plowing with a two-bottom sulky plow.
Photo by Kim Zeazel.

Gail Deets with Maude and Molly on the side delivery rake at his Old Fashioned Horsefarming Day. Photo by Kim Yeazel.

Tom Hagemann takes the lines for a demonstration of hay loading. There are four people on the wagon, but only two were necessary — the teamster and the stacker. The "one man loader" wagon contains a conveyor in the wagon bed and a ratchet (seen behind the man with the black shirt) which enabled the stacker to move the entire load forward on the wagon by a pull of the ratchet lever. In this way only one man was needed to do the stacking, as it only had to be stacked at the back of the wagon, under the loader.

John Elliot brought a foal along, and before the day was over the foal was learning how to mow hay. Both photos by Rick Miller.

Marc Gravert is always busy at Gail's field day. Above he is doing some plowing with his walking plow, and at the left his team in on a horsepower. The horsepower is driving an elevator which is carrying corn into the corncrib. Both photos by Kim Yeazel.

Uwe Schultz brought some of his Belgians to the 1992 Old Fashioned Horsefarming Day. With him on the grain drill is his son, Ernest. Both photos by Rick Miller.

Merle Fischer of Jefferson, Wisconsin, hosted a spring field day sponsored by the Jefferson County Draft Horse Club. Here he is plowing with six Percheron geldings. Merle took the idea that this is a show seriously, using his fancy spotted harness and show bridles and housings.

Chuck Hansell of Columbus, Wisconsin, plowing some cornstalk stubble with his team of Clydes.

Gordy Lieurance (Delavan, Wisconsin) raises and exhibits Welsh ponies, but he also showed he could also handle big horses by driving Wayne Randall's blacks on this big disc. The two inside horses are tied together, and Gordy has lines to the outside of all four horses.

151

The fall field day for the Northern Minnesota Draft Horse Association attracted over 100 horses and about 1,100 spectators. Among the horses was this team of greys which pulled a wagon filled with spectators around the Robert Blomberg farm where the field day was held. This team is owned by Arlyn and Leonna Westerberg of Amery, Wisconsin, and was driven during the field day by Don Carlson, also of Amery.

Scenes like this occur over and over again at field days. Grandpa is explaining something to the grandchildren, and the children just stand in awe of these big horses. The team belongs to David Stalheim.

Dennis Oehrlein from Brainered, Minnesota, brought his Teamster 2000 forecart to the Minnesota Field Day. Here he is pulling a corn binder with his three Percherons. The binder is being powered by the ground-driven power-take-off on the forecart. The bundles are conveyed up the elevator and being loaded on a wagon pulled by a team of Clydesdales owned and driven by David Stalheim.

Earlier in the day Dennis had his team of blacks hooked to a ground-driven corn binder.

One of the highlights of the Minnesota field day was when Bruce Coen of Luck, Wisconsin, hooked twelve Belgians to a 4-bottom (14") gang plow. All twelve horses belonged to Bruce, and almost all were home-grown.

Two views of teamsters from the Iowa-Minnesota Draft Horse Association bringing in bundles of oats to the threshing machine. At the top we see Norton Johnson of Harmony, Minnesota, with his team of Percheron mares. To the left we see Sandy Schott of West Union, Iowa, with his Belgian team in fly nets.

The organizers of the field days take special pains to demonstrate as many activities as possible. Here Randy and Don Denton of Barnum, Minnesota, demonstrate road building by operating a road grader in the middle of the field.

The Iowa-Minnesota Draft Horse Association had their 1993 Annual Fall Horse Plowing Contest at Decorah, Iowa. This six up of Belgians on a two-bottom sulky plow was owned and driven by Merle Monroe of Castalia, Iowa.

157

It was a real traffic-stopper when three binders were working in the same field in July, 1994, as the Iowa-Minnesota Draft Horse Association cut the oats on a field near Decorah, Iowa. Leading this group is Judson Schrick followed by Bob Pietan and Merle Monroe.

Normally the goal at a field day is to show how things were done, using horses, many years ago. Quite a different type of field day was held on the Elmer Lapp farm in Lancaster County, Pennsylvania, in June, 1994. This day, sponsored by the Draft Horse & Mule Association, had demonstrations of modern farming machinery and techniques using horses (and mules) instead of tractors. Above we see four horses pulling a modern liquid manure spreader, this time filled with water pumped from a stream, instead of manure, for demonstration purposes.

We will close with another scene from the first Draft Horse and Mule Agricultural Progress Days held in June, 1994, in Lancaster County, Pennsylvania. Here we have four horses hooked to a forecart pulling a gasoline-powered kick-baler. Actually, anytime you might visit Lancaster County you will see modern tillage, cultivating, and harvesting equipment being pulled and moved by horses and mules. The entire area is a living, breathing demonstration of how to combine old fashioned horsepower with modern farming methods.

INDEX OF PEOPLE FEATURED IN THIS BOOK